# Seaside

# Sen

Paul Humphrey

Photography by Chris Fairclough

## W
## FRANKLIN WATTS
LONDON•SYDNEY

First published in 2006 by
Franklin Watts
338 Euston Road
London NW1 3BH

Franklin Watts Australia
Hachette Children's Books
Level 17/207 Kent Street
Sydney NSW 2000

© 2006 Franklin Watts

ISBN: 0 7496 6610 2 (hbk)
ISBN: 0 7496 6854 7 (pbk)

Dewey classification number: 612.8

Planning and production by Discovery Books Limited
Editor: Rachel Tisdale
Designer: Ian Winton
Photography: Chris Fairclough
Series advisors: Diana Bentley MA and Dee Reid MA,
Fellows of Oxford Brookes University

The author, packager and publisher would like to thank the following
people for their participation in this book: Auriel Austin-Baker; Arrandeep Bola
and family; Lucas Tisdale.

Printed in China

# Contents

# Seaside senses

At the seaside, there are lots of things to see, hear...

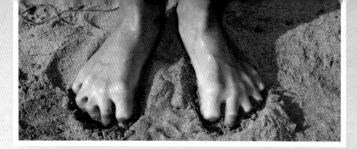

...smell, touch and taste.

5

# Beach huts and kites

You can see beach huts painted in bright colours...

...and a kite flying
in the breeze.

# Shells and pebbles

Look at the colours
of the shells
and pebbles.

9

# Crashing waves

You can hear waves rolling onto the shore...

...or crashing on
the rocks.

11

# Seaside sounds

You can hear a seagull calling...

...and people laughing
and shouting.

# Seaside smells

You can smell
seaweed...

...and fish and chips!

# Rough and smooth

The rocks feel rough.

But the pebbles
are smooth.

# Cold and hot

The sea feels
so cold...

# ...but the sun is hot.

19

# Wind and sand

You can feel the wind in your hair...

...and the sand
under your feet.

# Salty and sweet

## The sea is salty...

...but ice cream tastes
lovely and sweet!

# Word bank

Look back for these words and pictures.

Beach huts

Ice cream

Kite

Pebbles

Rocks

Seagull

Seaweed

Shells

Waves

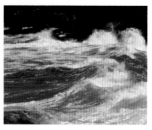